W9-CYE-626

THE UPSTREAM JOURNEY OF
SALMON

BY ANNETTE GULATI

Published by The Child's World®
1980 Lookout Drive • Mankato, MN 56003-1705
800-599-READ • www.childsworld.com

Photographs ©: Mark Caunt/Shutterstock Images, cover, 1; Menno Schaefer/
Shutterstock Images, 5; iStockphoto, 6, 11, 12; National Park Service, 8;
PerfectStills/iStockphoto, 9; Murphy Shewchuk/iStockphoto, 13; Shutterstock
Images, 14; Lynn Bystrom/iStockphoto, 16; Minden Pictures/SuperStock, 17;
Roland Hemmi/ImageBROKER/Glow Images, 18; E. Peter Steenstra/U.S. Fish
and Wildlife Service, 20

ISBN 9781503816237

LCCN 2016945666

Printed in the United States of America
PA02319

TABLE OF
CONTENTS

FAST FACTS 4

Chapter 1
HEADING HOME 7

Chapter 2
PAST THE DAM........................ 11

Chapter 3
FARTHER UPSTREAM 15

Chapter 4
HOME AGAIN!......................... 19

Think About It 21
Glossary 22
To Learn More 23
Selected Bibliography 23
Index 24
About the Author 24

FAST FACTS

Name

- There are eight types of Pacific salmon: Chinook, coho, sockeye, chum, pink, steelhead, masu, and amago.

Diet

- Young salmon eat insects, **invertebrates**, and **plankton**.
- Adult salmon eat other fish, squid, eel, and shrimp.

Average Life Span

- Most salmon live for four to five years.
- Chinook salmon live the longest. They live up to seven years.

Size

- Adult pink salmon are as small as 20 inches (51 cm) long.
- Chinook salmon can grow up to 5 feet (1.5 m) long.

Weight

- Pink salmon weigh as little as 3 to 5 pounds (1.4–2.3 kg).

- Chinook salmon can weigh as much as 100 pounds (45 kg).

Where They're Found

- Salmon live in the Atlantic and Pacific Oceans.

- Some salmon also live in inland lakes, such as the Great Lakes.

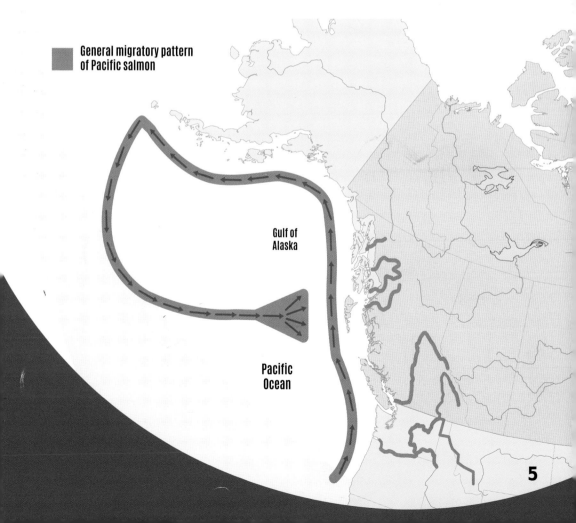

General migratory pattern of Pacific salmon

Gulf of Alaska

Pacific Ocean

Chapter 1

HEADING HOME

It is early September. A female salmon has spent three years in the Pacific Ocean. It is time to leave. She will return to the place she was born. Where she was born is a good place to **spawn**. She begins her long journey home to Washington State.

The salmon swims south. She finds a body of water called an **estuary**. This is where a river meets the ocean. The salmon stays here for several weeks. The mix of salt water and freshwater in the estuary prepares her to live in the river. New muscles develop that will help her sprint and jump. Eggs start to grow in her body. The salmon gobbles down a few more fish. This will be the last meal of her life.

◄ After living most of their lives in the ocean, salmon return to the freshwater rivers from which they came.

▲ Salmon's bodies quickly adapt to allow them to take in freshwater instead of salt water.

Soon the salmon is ready to leave. She finds the mouth of the river and heads upstream. Many other salmon join her. The **current** is strong. She pushes against it with her tail and fins. She must move her body quickly to swim up the river. She leaps over rocks. She jumps over logs. The salmon run has begun!

The salmon arrives at a deep pool. A waterfall 10 feet (3 m) tall splashes into the pool. There is no other way to move up the river. The salmon must go up the waterfall.

She dives down to the depths of the pool and then swims upward. She swings her tail fin and springs into the air. The water from the waterfall pushes down on the salmon. She flops back into the river. She rests for a few minutes. Then she tries again. This time she makes it!

▲ Some salmon can leap over obstacles 12 feet (4 m) high.

Chapter 2

PAST THE DAM

The female salmon leaves the waterfall behind. The clouds darken. Rain pours down and the river rises. The salmon swims hard. Her body is shaped like a cylinder. This makes her a fast swimmer. She can swim against strong currents.

The salmon approaches **rapids**. Along with other salmon, she dives over them. Her body scrapes against a rock. It does not hurt her. Her shiny **scales** protect her. They are like a suit of armor.

Soon the female salmon reaches a **dam**. It blocks her way upstream. A sea lion barks. He sits at the base of the dam, waiting for a meal. The sea lion slides off the rock into the water. He swims toward her.

◄ Salmon must swim through shallow areas, called riffles, in rivers and streams.

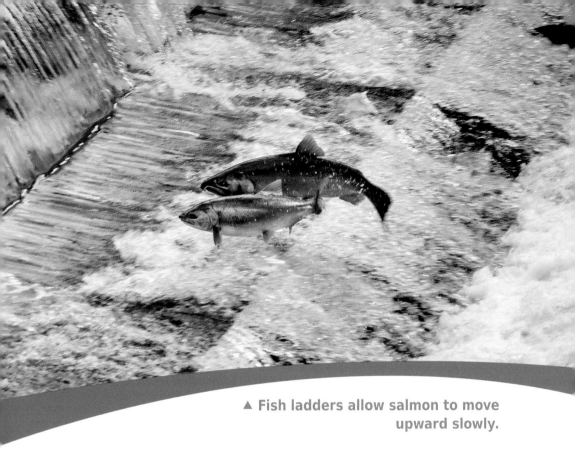

▲ Fish ladders allow salmon to move upward slowly.

The salmon dodges left, then right. Quickly, she escapes. Another salmon is not so lucky.

Next the salmon hears bubbling water nearby. She darts toward it. It is a fish ladder. Fish ladders help salmon get past dams. The salmon leaps into the rushing water. She lands in a small pool. She jumps again. Step by step, she inches her way up the ladder. She rests when she gets tired. Finally the salmon has made it up and over the dam.

The salmon does not stop swimming. On and on she goes. She will travel more than 300 miles (480 km). She is not alone. Thousands of salmon swim with her. All the fish are returning to the creeks where they were born.

▲ Salmon's bodies change as they migrate. Sockeye salmon turn bright red.

Chapter 3

FARTHER UPSTREAM

It has been a long, hot summer. Upstream, the river feels warm. The female salmon slows down. Soil has washed into the water. It is dark and muddy. She prefers cold, clean water. She struggles to get oxygen from the warm water.

Trash lies near the river's edge. It floats on the surface. Chemicals flow downstream from a nearby city. The salmon is in danger. She could catch a disease. But **mucus** covers her scales. This slimy coating protects her from getting sick.

She pushes herself farther. She comes to a fork in the river. Some other salmon swim to the left.

◄ **Pollution can make a salmon's migration even more difficult.**

▲ Migrating salmon provide an important source of food for black bears and other woodland animals.

The female salmon smells something familiar the other direction. She swims up the smaller river to the right.

The river narrows. It flows into a cool mountain lake. The salmon glides along in the shallow water near shore. A hungry black bear wades into the water. The river is red with salmon. The bear pounces into the water. The female salmon darts away from the bear's snout.

The salmon has narrowly missed getting eaten by the bear. Still she is in poor shape. She has lost weight.

Her fin is torn. She no longer has her mucus coating. White fungus grows on her side. She has developed a disease. She uses the stored energy from her fat to keep swimming.

One morning, the female salmon enters a creek. Trees shade the pale blue water. Stones line the bottom. She recognizes the smell in the water. Three weeks after she began, her journey has ended. She is back home!

▲ If a salmon loses the layer of mucus on its skin, it can develop diseases.

Chapter 4

HOME AGAIN!

The female salmon is ready to lay her eggs. She chooses a shallow spot in the gravelly stream. First she bends her body into a U shape. She begins digging a hole with her tail. It takes her a few hours. When she is done, her nest can be 7 to 20 inches (18–51 cm) deep. The nest is called a redd.

Two male salmon notice her. They want to **fertilize** her eggs. They bite each other with their sharp teeth. They slap each other with their tails. One salmon swims away. The stronger male wins. He will fertilize the female's eggs.

The female rests on the bottom of the stream. She immediately lays her eggs in the redd she dug.

◀ Salmon clear away small rocks that could get pushed away with the current. This makes their nests more stable.

▲ Baby salmon swim after hatching. Very few salmon live long enough to reproduce and migrate.

The eggs look like orange-red balls. Each one is as tiny as a pea. The male swims up next to her. He releases a liquid. The eggs are fertilized. The female salmon wants to keep the eggs safe. She rakes her tail back and forth. She covers the eggs with gravel.

Next the female salmon swims a little way up the stream. She digs another redd and lays more eggs.

Each time, the male fertilizes them. The female salmon digs four redds. In all, she lays 10,000 eggs. It takes her three days to lay all of the eggs.

It is time to rest. Both salmon are tired. The female stays close to her redds. Laying eggs is hard work. The upstream journey has also been hard. One week later, both the male and female salmon die. Their bodies drift downstream. The eggs are now on their own. Fewer than ten of the fish inside the eggs will live to be adults. Someday those adults will return to the same creek. They will make the same journey as their parents.

THINK ABOUT IT

- What do you think is the greatest danger salmon face on their journey?
- How is the salmon's life different from other fish and animals?
- If you could invent something that would make a salmon's life easier, what would it be?

GLOSSARY

current (KUR-uhnt): Current is the movement of water in rivers, streams, and oceans. Salmon swim against the current to find a spot to lay their eggs.

dam (DAM): A dam is a structure that blocks the flow of water. Salmon must get past a dam to continue up the river.

estuary (ES-choo-er-ee): An estuary is a body of water where the ocean meets the river. The salmon stay in the estuary before swimming upstream.

fertilize (FUR-tuh-lize): To fertilize is to make an egg ready to hatch. Male salmon fertilize the female salmon's eggs.

invertebrates (in-VUR-tuh-brits): Invertebrates are animals without backbones. Salmon eat small invertebrates.

mucus (MYOO-cuss): Mucus is a thick liquid that protects parts of the body. Mucus covers a salmon's scales.

plankton (PLANGK-tuhn): Plankton are tiny plants and animals floating in the water. Young salmon eat plankton.

rapids (RAP-idz): Rapids are part of a river where the water flows very quickly. Salmon must be strong to swim through the rapids.

scales (SKAYLZ): Scales are thin, overlapping plates that cover a salmon's body. Scales protect the salmon from harm.

spawn (SPAWN): To spawn is to produce young, usually in large numbers. Salmon swim up the river to spawn.

TO LEARN MORE

Books

Harasymiw, Mark. *The Bizarre Life Cycle of a Salmon*. New York: Gareth Stevens, 2013.

Miller, Debbie S., and John H. Eiler. *A King Salmon Journey*. Fairbanks, AK: U of Alaska, 2014.

Sexton, Colleen A. *The Life Cycle of a Salmon*. Minneapolis, MN: Bellwether Media, 2010.

Web Sites

Visit our Web site for links about salmon:

childsworld.com/links

Note to Parents, Teachers, and Librarians: We routinely verify our Web links to make sure they are safe and active sites. So encourage your readers to check them out!

SELECTED BIBLIOGRAPHY

"Basic Facts about Salmon." *Defenders of Wildlife*. Defenders of Wildlife, 29 Feb. 2012. Web. 13 Jun. 2016.

Behnke, Robert J., and Joseph R. Tomelleri. *Trout and Salmon of North America*. New York: Free, 2002. Print.

"Pacific Salmon." *WorldWildlife.org*. World Wildlife Fund, n.d. Web. 13 Jun. 2016.

"Salmon of the West—What Is a Salmon?" *FWS.gov*. U.S. Fish & Wildlife Service, n.d. Web. 13 Jun. 2016.

INDEX

bears, 16

chemicals, 15
current, 8, 11

dam, 11–12

eggs, 7, 19–21
estuary, 7

fat, 17
fertilize, 19–21
fish ladder, 12
freshwater, 7
fungus, 17

jump, 7–8, 12

lake, 5, 16

mucus, 15, 17
muscles, 7

plankton, 4

rapids, 11
redd, 19–21
rivers, 7–9, 11, 15–16

scales, 11, 15
sea lion, 11
spawn, 7

trash, 15

Washington State, 7

waterfall, 8–9, 11

ABOUT THE AUTHOR

Annette Gulati is a freelance writer and children's author living in Seattle, Washington. She has published stories, articles, essays, poems, crafts, and activities in numerous magazines, newspapers, and anthologies. She also writes books for children's educational publishers.